The ELGIN or CHARLESTOWN RAILWAY
1762-1863

Early Colliery Wagon from a contemporary illustration
Elgin Archives

DUNCAN McNAUGHTON, MA FSA Scot.

Thomas, 7th Earl of Elgin and 11th Earl of Kincardine 1766-1841. The only known portrait c1793.

By permission of the Earl of Elgin. (Tom Scott)

CONTENTS

FOREWORD

by

The Right Hon. The Earl of Elgin and Kincardine, KT DL JP

In a long letter dated 20 April 1755, written at Broomhall by Janet, Countess of Kincardine, to her son, Charles, Earl of Elgin and Kincardine, and received by him in Paris on 2 May, one of several telling phrases reads thus:

> *The more I think of your project of a draw kiln for burning your lime I like it the worse, for the kiln must be built and then it will employ six men and upward of 20 carriages of coals at 2 miles distance every day, all these must be hired by the year that the work stand not idle.*

Lady Kincardine's fears were, on Lord Elgin's return to Scotland in 1757, rapidly resolved. He built not one but six kilns, laid out a village of some 200 houses, created a small harbour on the shore of the Firth of Forth below the village, and set several hundred men to work, quarrying lime from the enormous limestone crag which jutted close by, along the North bank of the river.

Nevertheless, Lady Kincardine had been correct in assessing the considerable quantities of coal required. This coal came from West and North of Dunfermline and was mainly the property of the Halketts of Pitfirrane: but several other landowners were also involved, and it was the building of the harbour which Lord Elgin felt could be an inducement to them all. Their coal was of little value unless it could be sold to a sea-borne trade; nor would they be able to improve their land by applying lime unless he could get a steady supply of coal with which to burn his rock.

What Mr. McNaughton now tells us is the fascinating story of how this problem was at first resolved by the building of a railed wagonway. The least of the difficulties was, in fact, the actual construction of the railway. Greater problems were to be found in the mutual distrust and cantankerous wrangling of the several proprietors through whose land the line was to pass; and, indeed neither of the two principal advocates of the idea profited personally from the completed works: Dr. Chalmers was, by then, bankrupt and Lord Elgin dead.

However, the wagonway was completed, and in running order, by 1774, and from its combined beginnings it became more and more the sole property of the Earls of Elgin, until it was just known as 'the

4

Elgin Railway'. As the decades pass, the story describes the alterations and improvements which were made. Wood gives place to iron, horses to ingenious inclined planes; stationary steam engines appear, and levels are again adjusted; and then, hesitantly, locomotive steam engines make their way along the line. Over nearly all the stages of development in the 19th century, the restless energy of the 7th Earl was a dominant feature. In 1802 he took the fateful decision to make a physical collection of marble sculptures in Athens, and he also wrote from Constantinople to authorise the acquisition of iron rails for the wagonway. He was, later, to engage the advice of a succesion of enterprising railway engineers, including Stephenson, and to travel in his locomotive-powered train - of which he did not approve, owing to its violent oscillation. A few years before he died, the 7th Earl designed, personally, an omnibus carriage to take passengers from Dunfermline to Charlestown. This was an inspired decision: thousands of passengers annually took advantage, of which possibly the most important in ultimate terms was the family of Andrew Carnegie, on their way to North America.

Three generations of Earls were closely connected with the development and maintenance of the line, until it was sold to the North British Railway Company and became a part of the national system even until today.

It may not have been the first, or the largest, railroad in Scotland, but to Dunfermline and district it was of enormous commercial value and, throughout the 90 years during which it was the property of Broomhall Estate, there grew up a community of railwaymen for whom it certainly provided a proud livelihood.

I am greatly indebted to Mr. MacNaughton for his thoroughgoing care in reading the mass of documents and letters which have survived, and in writing the story which the Carnegie Dunfermline Trustees have so generously agreed to publish.

PREFACE

The Charlestown to Dunfermline Railway, better known in its day as the Elgin Railway, has almost been forgotten, although it once played a major part in the industrial development of Dunfermline and District in the late 18th and the first half of the 19th centuries. There have been several short references to it in print but, because the papers and records pertaining to it were not then available, these accounts are superficial and not always accurate.

Through the courtesy and encouragement of the Earl of Elgin, a large number of documents relating to the founding and operation of the railway has been collected from his archives to allow a more detailed history of the railway to be written, covering the period 1762-1863. No doubt much still remains to be unearthed, but apart from providing additional details, future discoveries will not substantially alter the present account.

As most of this account of an aspect of the industrial history of West Fife has been based on unpublished material, made up of private correspondence of the Earls of Elgin, lawyers' letters, counsels' opinions, factors' and managers' reports, as well as surveyors' and engineers' sketches, it has not been possible, nor thought desirable, to give references except where essential, as this account was written for the general reader with an interest in local history. However, all the documents relating to the railway are now catalogued for the benefit of any future researchers.

It has not been found possible to include in the illustrations any official maps of the early railway, for such never existed, but there are several large-scale plans, mainly dating from the period after 1863 when the railway had been acquired by the North British Railway Co., which are too large to be suitably reduced. These are to be found in the North British Railway Co. archives in the West Register House, Edinburgh, under the references S.C.P.631 for the whole railway 1858, R.H.P.15819 being a section of the Pittencrieff incline 1876, and R.H.P. 15821 showing a detailed plan of the track and sidings there in 1868.

I am indebted to Lord Elgin for permission to use the information from his archives, and for many valuable suggestions and clarifications from his extensive knowledge of the history of his family and estate.

I would also thank Mr. Miller for painstakingly photocopying documents and illustrations, and bearing with my requests for assistance over a long period. Many thanks are also due to Mr. Norman Clark for drawing the outline map and to the staff of the Carnegie Central Library, Dunfermline, for their willing co-operation in tracing references.

Above all, I am deeply indebted to the Carnegie Dunfermline Trust for word-processing the original manuscript and making this publication possible.

DUNCAN McNAUGHTON, MA, FSA Scot.

Dunfermline 1986

THE ELGIN OR CHARLESTOWN RAILWAY
1762 - 1863

The Background

The Elgin Railway owed its existence and its importance in the industrial and agricultural development of the area around Dunfermline to the fact that, as a result of the discoveries and inventions of the Industrial Revolution leading to the rise of the iron industry, there arose an insatiable demand for suitable coal for smelting, as well as fuel for the new steam engines on sea and land. In addition, improvements in agriculture had created a similar demand for lime by farmers and landowners throughout Scotland. Both coal and lime could be found in abundance in the Dunfermline area.

Long before the 18th century coal was being worked in shallow mines on Abbey lands, the first recorded date being 1291, when William de Oberville, then in Pittencrieff, granted the monks the right to mine coal on his lands for their own use. At the Reformation in 1560, we find the Wellwoods of Touch being confirmed in their possession of coal workings on Abbey lands at Baldridge and Touch. Farther to the west of the town, the Halkett family at Pitfirrane had developed such extensive workings on their estate that in 1563 they were granted the right to export the coal free of customs, a right renewed by Queen Anne in 1706, ratified by Parliament in 1707, and retained until 1788. Part of the Halkett lands lay to the north of Dunfermline, and their mines around Balmule were leased to the Wellwoods in the latter half of the 18th century.

The Town Council of Dunfermline was also mining coal at an early date. In 1670 the town came to an arrangement with the Earl of Dunfermline and the Earl of Tweeddale to take over or commence the mining of coal on the Town Muir near Townhill. This was still being carried on well into the 19th century but by that time the bulk of that coal was being sent via the Halbeath wagonway to St. Davids.

By the end of the 18th century new and improved methods of ventilation, drainage, and haulage had led to deeper seams being exploited, so that greater production could meet the increasing demand of a growing iron industry. Most of this output had to be sent by sea, mainly from the Halkett port of Brucehaven near the village of Limekilns (which itself had a form of harbour), because the roads were primitive and often impassable in bad weather. There

9

was thus an urgent need for an improvement in the system of transportation from the coalfield to the Forth.

The second factor in the industrial history of the area was the demand for lime. Limestone deposits had always been exploited at Limekilns as its name indicates, but only in a relatively small way, and mainly for building purposes. As the Agricultural Revolution of the 18th century gained momentum, the market for lime for field dressing expanded rapidly, and Charles, 5th Earl of Elgin, began to extend his limestone quarries near Broomhall, where he built new kilns before 1760.

To provide an outlet he constructed a harbour and founded the village of Charlestown in 1761, partly to provide for his workers and partly to provide facilities for ships' crews waiting for a tide. Now coasting vessels could load at a quay instead of having to lie out in the river and be loaded from small boats which had picked up the limestone from the beach to which it had been rolled down from the quarries. New and improved kilns were planned by the 5th Earl, though much of the construction did not take place until after his death in 1771.

Lime burning required large quantitites of suitable coal, but at this period there were no workable deposits on the Broomhall estate, and Lord Elgin had to be dependent on supplies brought down from the Pitfirrane mines around Knockhouse and Urqhart, as well as from other Pitfirrane-owned coal deposits at Baldridge near Dunfermline, and Balmule to the north of the town, rented by Robert Wellwood of Garvock and Pitliver. Other supplies came from mines on Pittencrieff. This meant a slow, cumbersome, and expensive haul over rough country roads by clumsy wagons drawn by two horses at least. Although short stretches of improved roads had been constructed, such as the Waggon Road at Crossford and the Pittencrieff Coal Road (the latter being the work of the Forbes family of Pittencrieff about 1759), the other roads to Brucehaven, Limekilns and Charlestown continued to be inadequate to cope with the increased demand for coal for the limeworks, as well as for export to other parts of Scotland.

Plans and Stratagems

At this period there were initially three landowners involved in the expansion of the coal mining industry in this part of Fife - Sir John Wedderburn of Gosforth, now of Pitfirrane, Robert Wellwood of Garvock and Pitliver, and Charles, 5th Earl of Elgin. The initiative

10

for improvement in transport came from Lord Elgin. As early as 1762 he was in correspondence with his two neighbours over the possibility of building a light railway or wagonway, on which wagons running on rails would carry greater loads more swiftly than on the existing roads and would also require fewer horses to draw them. The idea of a wagonway was not new, for a similar tramway had been in operation between Cockenzie and Tranent as early as 1722 and others were being constructed by mid-century (Note 1).

The proposal was the subject of some desultory correspondence and discussion among the parties concerned, but for various reasons little was done, although Lord Elgin was gradually acquiring land between his house at Broomhall and Dunfermline as far as Gallowridge and the foot of the Pittencrieff Coal Road, showing that he envisaged a railway direct to the main coal deposits around the town. A number of undated plans and surveys preserved at Broomhall, together with estimates of feu duties for way-leave, may belong to this period, although they are more likely to have been drawn up for his son Thomas, 7th Earl of Elgin, who eventually constructed a wagonway along this route at the end of the century.

There were several factors inhibiting the progress of the actual construction of wagonway. In the first place, Sir John Wedderburn, who had inherited the name, estate, and baronetcy of Halkett of Pitfirrane on the death of Sir Peter Halkett and his heir at the battle of Fort Duquesne in America in 1755, had had his inheritance disputed in the courts, and it was not until 1769 that the case was decided in his favour.

Only then, as Sir John Halkett, could he authorise any major construction in connection with his estate. Now he had an additional incentive to improve his haulage, for he had leased the Urquhart coal from Sir Gilbert Elliot, as the mines there had become unworkable unless drained through the Pitfirrane level. Balmule coal, leased to Robert Wellwood, also required better haulage facilities.

The second and main stumbling block, however, was George Chalmers (Note 2), who had bought Pittencrieff estate just before 1765. A successful Edinburgh corn merchant, Chalmers obviously intended to make his purchase a profitable investment by developing its potential as a coal producing area, for it extended over parts of Baldridge and westwards towards Luscar. To assist his plan he leased the port of Brucehaven from Sir John Wedderburn, as at this time it was the main outlet for coal from the Dunfermline mines. Early in 1765, almost as soon as he was installed in Pittencrieff, Chalmers suggested to Lord Elgin that a direct wagonway should be built between Dunfermline and Brucehaven. To further this, he had already signed a missive to acquire a portion of Gallowridge on the proposed route, and in 1768 had actually entered into a contract to purchase the remainder from John Thomson, who then owned the farm. Apparently at this point he had intended to build the wagonway himself, but now abandoned this scheme in favour of another, by which Lord Elgin would build it at his own expense in return for favourable freight charges and the guarantee of a regular supply of Mr. Chalmer's coal. The change of plan was probably due to the fact that, belatedly, Chalmers realised that Lord Elgin had already acquired by purchase or lease most of the land through which such a wagonway would pass, and that he would then have to pay for the way-leave. Not only did he relinquish to Lord Elgin his contract to buy Gallowridge, but also allowed him to take a lease in 1767 of the Kerse of Pittencrieff, the level ground at the foot of the Coal Road. Lord Elgin also acquired the Hole, a small holding near Leggats Bridge, in 1769 when he finally bought Gallowridge. Thus by that date Lord Elgin could build a wagonway as far as the Pittencrieff Coal Road on his own land.

Meanwhile, although he agreed with Chalmers' original proposal to provide a regular supply of coal from the Pittencrieff mines, Lord Elgin had admitted his friends, Robert Wellwood of Garvock and Pitliver, and Sir John Halkett of Pitfirrane, to share the benefits of the projected wagonway. Chalmers objected strongly, as he had discovered that they had abandoned the idea of a direct line from Dunfermline to Brucehaven or Limekilns in favour of a plan for an alternative wagonway to run from Urquhart to provide a line through Pitfirrane to Limekilns. Thus Limekilns and not Brucehaven, now leased by Chalmers, would be confirmed as the main coal-exporting port on the Forth. It was also a route which would serve Lord Elgin's limeworks better than one terminating at Brucehaven.

Chalmers was thus faced with having to build his own line to Brucehaven and pay feu duties to Lord Elgin, or pay for freight charges via Pitfirrane. His response was to attempt to come to an agreement with Lord Elgin which specifically excluded Wellwood and Halkett, whom he also attempted to buy out of any commitment they had already entered into with Lord Elgin. These gentlemen were now well aware of Chalmers' real intentions, as Sir John Wedderburn (now Sir John Halkett) revealed in a letter to Lord Elgin on 26th January 1770, in which he quoted part of a letter he had received from Chalmers in July of the previous year. Chalmers had written:

You are pleased frequently in company to be complaining of the high rate you and Mr. Wellwood are to pay me of way-leave for the intended wagonroad. I am so much of different opinion as to this rate, that if ever the Contract between the Earl of Elgin and me is carried into execution, I shall be willing to give you and Mr. Wellwood five hundred guineas to relinquish the option you have of a share therein and which I hope you will have the candour to mention in the future when you have occasion to complain of the high rate.

Sir John went on to comment:

This proof that all his complaints about Mr. Wellwood and myself of going off at your point of Partition (i.e. branching off to Urquhart) *are ill-grounded, or rather that his grand scheme (which his proposal to your Lordship to give you £500 not to admit us made pretty evident) was to make a monopoly of the wholl coal in this part of the country by rendering the carriage of Mr. Wellwood's coal and mine so high to the sea that it would not be much to our advantage to work them, and that then he might make an easy purchase of them. This appears from all his transactions in this affair to have been his great object.*

Finally, having failed in his plan, Chalmers obtained an injunction suspending all contracts with Lord Elgin, and forbidding any attempt to construct a wagonway through his estate. This action decided Lord Elgin and his friends to consider an alternative route to the sea, one which had already been considered as an extension of the proposed wagonway through Urquhart and Pitfirrane. Indeed in 1769 a contract had actually been signed between Lord Elgin and Sir John Halkett to build a wagonway from Crossford and Knockhouse across Broomhall estate to Limekilns pier. (Unfortunately no trace of this contract has been found). For the time being the direct route was in abeyance, although Chalmers returned to the proposal in 1776, admitting the 7th Earl of Elgin and the others on the same terms. This was ignored by the young Earl's Trustees (Charles, Lord Elgin had died in 1771). Circumstances had changed. A wagonway had been constructed and Chalmers was no longer in a position to put pressure on the other coal owners. In fact he had over-reached himself by building a bridge across the Tower Burn at the foot of Dunfermline High Street and opening up new streets on the opposite bank, with the result that, although the main road into Dunfermline was removed from the vicinity of Pittencrieff House, he bankrupted himself, and his lands and leases underwent a judicial sale in 1785. Most of his coal bearing areas were eventually bought by Thomas, 7th Lord Elgin (Note 3).

The Original Wagonway

As stated above, circumstances had changed by the time Chalmers made his last attempt to secure an outlet for his coal. Charles, 5th Earl of Elgin, died in 1771 without seeing his plans for a railway to his lime kilns and harbour materialising. His eldest son, William, the 6th Earl, died within a few months of his father, to be succeeded by his younger brother, Thomas the 7th Earl, a boy of five. As he was a minor, Tutors or Trustees had to be appointed to manage the estate until he came of age. The most influential of these, and virtual managing director of the activities of the estate, was his mother, Martha, Dowager Countess of Elgin. Born Martha Whyte of Kirkcaldy, she was the daughter of Thomas Whyte, a member of a prominent Kirkcaldy family and a merchant in Kirkcaldy and London, and was in high favour with George III and his family, becoming, after her husband's death, Governess to the Royal children. She resided mainly at Windsor or Downing Street, but found time to write weekly, sometimes daily, to John Grant, factor at Broomhall, issuing instructions and demanding reports. She was largely responsible for a policy of tree planting, and for extensions to the lime kilns, while finding time to take notice of the conduct and welfare of the house and estate servants. Her voluminous but uncatalogued correspondence would reveal a fascinating picture of social and political events in the latter years of the 18th Century.

During the minority of the young Earl, however, the Trustees had to be careful not to involve the estate in a great deal of capital expenditure such as the building of a railway, although they were not opposed to the project, realising how advantageous it might be in the long run.

Lord Elgin's death had prevented the implementation of the contract to build signed in 1769, though the Trustees were willing to allow Sir John Halkett to proceed at his own expense. By 1772 Sir John had leased his coal workings to William Cadell and Company, formed by William Cadell, one of the founders of Carron Ironworks, his two sons, William and John, and John Beaumont of Newcastle, one of a family long involved in the development of mining in West Fife. This company was not only supplying Carron Ironworks, but was soon exporting cargoes of Pitfirrane coal to Amsterdam in an expanding Continental market (Cadell Papers).

To facilitate increased deliveries to Limekilns harbour and Lord Elgin's expanding limeworks, William Cadell began a survey of the route for the wagonway agreed on in 1769. This was to be built by his company, at their own expense, on ground leased for fourteen

14

years, after which the track was to be removed, unless the Earl of Elgin desired to acquire its lease and operate the railway himself. Some construction had apparently been done before 1772 when a dispute with the Elgin Trustees halted the wagonway on the boundary of Broomhall estate (see Ainslie's map of 1775). Apparently (details are lacking) Cadell & Co wished to make changes in the agreed route, to which the Trustees objected unless a greatly increased feu duty of £5-5/- per acre was paid for the ground occupied by the track as it crossed the estate, a sum which appears excessive.

After much legal wrangling, correspondence and arbitration, agreement was finally reached, enabling the wagonway to be completed and in operation by the end of 1774. Neither the Cadell papers in the National Library (from which much of the above account was obtained) nor the Elgin archives have revealed the deviation intended or the terms of settlement, although the eventual route was closer to Broomhall House, slightly west of the projected track shown on Ainslie's map.

In 1774, with deliveries ensured by the new railway from Pitfirrane to Limekilns, Cadell entered into a new lease of the Pitfirrane coalmines. For the whole of the coal from Knockhouse, Pitconnochie and Luscar Eviot (now Lochhead), the coal depot at Limekilns pier, and all the collier houses connected with the workings, Cadell agreed to pay an annual rent of £1,000 with an additional £50 for any ironstone which might be discovered in the mining operations, which was an extremely high sum considering the value of money at the period.

The lease does not seem to have been profitable, for within a few years it was sold to a member of the Beaumont family, who complained bitterly to William Cadell that he had been grossly misled as to the profitability of the undertaking, and that as a result he was being reduced to bankruptcy. Eventually about 1786, Thomas 7th Earl of Elgin assumed the leases of the Pitfirrane coal and of the wagonway. The former was retained well into the 19th century despite a long and expensive law suit over what was permitted to be extracted.

The only contemporary map or plan of this first wagonway is Ainslie's map of West Fife of 1775. It appears to have been surveyed no later than 1772, as it shows only the first completed section of the railway as far as the Broomhall boundary. The remainder is shown as a projected route towards Limekilns. As delineated on this map the route appears to be slightly too far to the east at its northern end as it crossed Keavil estate and continued parallel to

Ainslie's map of 1775 showing the original wagonway from Knockhill to Limekilns. There is no evidence to show that it extended as far as Berrylaw.

Dunfermline District Library

the present Crossford Waggon Road. It is interesting to note that, while it is recorded that the wagonway served primarily the Knockhouse mines north of Crossford, the map indicates that it commenced farther to the north-east at Urquhart and Berrylaw nearer Pittencrieff and Baldridge. No confirmation of this has been found in the existing records, and it looks suspiciously like the route proposed for the projected alternative to Chalmers' direct line which was never implemented. It is possible that the mapmaker, knowing that it would be some time before this map would be published, had assumed that the railway being planned around 1770 would in fact be built following that route. If this map is accurate, it is unlikely that Lord Elgin would have entered into discussions in 1795 with William Hunt of Urquhart to build another railway in such close proximity to one already in existence.

Starting at Knockhouse (or beyond) the new wagonway ran south south-east parallel to the present Waggon Road at Crossford, passing between Meadowend and Craigs Bank until slightly north-east of Sillieton, north of Broomhall, it swung south-eastwards to cross Broomhall estate about a field's breadth in front of Broomhall House. Thereafter it turned towards Limekilns parallel to the Limekilns Road, behind the present bungalows on the right of that road. Reaching the village it ran through the Old Orchard to reach Limekilns pier. Limekilns remained the main coal exporting port until Charlestown took its place with the building of an extension of the wagonway to Charlestown in 1799. No technical details of the first wagonway seem to have survived, even if they were ever available, for a government report on the railway in 1853 notes that they were not then in existence. Nevertheless it is possible to glean a few details from various isolated letters and rough notes by Thomas, Lord Elgin, probably dating from a period around 1812 when the new line to Dunfermline was being built. In accordance with the original agreement of 1769 he appears to have taken a new lease of the railway by 1786 at the end of the original fourteen years period, and in 1799 he had built a spur down to Charlestown to a point above the harbour, behind the present Estate Office. From this terminus the wagons ran down through a cutting and tunnel to the quay, the laden wagons pulling up the empties on an endless rope. This was referred to as a 'gravity incline' or an 'inclined plane', and the principle was to be used later at the Dunfermline end of the later railway.

From Lord Elgin's notes and correspondence, we learn that until 1811 the wagons ran on wooden rails, resting on wooden sleepers, while the track was levelled by cuttings or embankments where necessary. The wagons in use were possibly similar to the cover illustration, which was described, in a fragile MS at Broomhall, as an ideal colliery wagon. (The MS gives a detailed description of its structure and dimensions.) It appears that this type had two cast iron wheels in front with concave rims or tyres, designed to keep the wagon on the rails. As the ballast was laid flush with the bottom of the rails, derailments were probably frequent. The system was an improvement however on earlier tracks elsewhere, where the wagons ran on iron plates laid on the ground.

Each of these wagons carried a load of 20 bolls, an old Scottish measure, roughly equivalent to a modern load of about 4½ tons, and required at least two horses to draw it. Stronger draught horses were required to assist at any incline. Most of the horses were kept at Charlestown, in stables opposite the present Sutlery, and even in the lower floor of that building, where huge vats were installed at the rear of the building to boil the potatoes which were believed to be ideal food for such horses.

The few rough notes in Lord Elgin's handwriting give a glimpse of the running costs of the wagonway and its branches within the lime works. They are undated but cannot be later than 1812, and seem to refer to the original railway which is described as being four miles in length. He also refers to another line from Townhill to Dunfermline which was three and a half miles long. Nothing has come to light which would connect this with his own line at this period, though there was a later extension of the Elgin Railway to Balmule colliery in the 1830s, built by Spowart of Venturefair.

The notes reveal that the maintenance of the wagonway, apart from wages, and the supply and upkeep of draught horses, was fairly expensive, considering the value of money at that time. In 1808, for example, the expenditure on timber for repair and replacement of wagons, rails and fencing amounted to £956:4/-, dropping in 1809 to £822:17:2. By 1810 the figure had risen to £1,979:14/-, which was almost equalled in the following year (Note 4). The sudden increase in expenditure was almost certainly due to the approaching completion of the new direct line from Charlestown to Dunfermline which was laid with iron rails. As these were fixed to stone blocks instead of wooden sleepers, the increased costs must have been largely due to the replacement of the earlier wagons by new ones suitable for iron rails. Though no references can be found, it is fairly certain that iron rails replaced the earlier wooden ones over the entire system, including the first wagonway and the branch lines into the pits and limeworks, as it is henceforth termed 'The Iron Railway' in the estate accounts and correspondence.

Charlestown to Pittencrieff

While the original wagonway, maintained and perhaps modernised, continued to operate well beyond the period envisaged in 1774, the possibility of implementing the original concept of a direct route to Dunfermline was never forgotten, and was apparently being considered from time to time, almost from the first years of the original track. In 1775, for example, the Trustees of Lord Elgin had a report prepared enumerating the feu duties involved in building such a railway by way of Gallowridge, and other documents - undated, but probably belonging to this period - detail actual measurements. A further investigation seems to have taken place after Thomas Lord Elgin had assumed control of the estate, resulting in several surveys of this route in the last decade of the century.

Throughout, only one possible line was envisaged, and was eventually adopted. This began at the head of the brae at Charlestown, and curved round by Merryhill, to turn east as it approached the foot of the Crossgates Waggon Road. Just beyond Sillieton, almost opposite Broomhall House, it turned north between Meadowend and Craigs Bank, passing west of Gallowridge, before bearing north east to reach a point near Leggats Bridge on the Dunfermline to Limekilns road from which it continued to the foot of the Coal Road. Despite the activity in costing and surveying in the latter years of the century, these plans were possibly not put into effect until 1795 or later.

Nevertheless in 1793 Lord Elgin had briefly returned to the scheme, originally suggested to his father by George Chalmers of Pittencrieff, of constructing a wagonway direct to Dunfermline, which would run through Pittencrieff parallel to the Coal Road to the Colton coal depot, to enable him to convey the coal from his mines beyond the Carnock Road, which now included those which had belonged to George Chalmers, as well as several workings in Baldridge leased from Pitfirrane. In 1793 therefore he signed a contract with Captain Phyn, who now owned Pittencrieff, to construct a railway or wagon road between Pittencrieff Toll, at the foot of the Coal Road, and the Coaltown of Pittencrieff or the Colton, which could then be extended beyond to Baldridge. Land for the track was actually delineated and allocated, but no feu duties were exacted by Pittencrieff, nor was any work ever started to implement the scheme. The report on Dunfermline in the Old Statistical Account states that Lord Elgin was already building a railway in this direction by 1795, which may suggest that the line was already being constructed from the Charlestown end, or that it refers to the extension of the existing line from Crossgates to Limekilns down to Charlestown harbour which was completed by 1799. The track and tunnel down the slope to the quays is still visible. Neither, however, is reflected in the estate accounts at this period so far as can be ascertained.

For some reason there was a change of policy before any major construction took place. Possibly it was realised that the two inclines towards the Colton presented a difficult engineering problem which might prove too costly, or that the outbreak of the French Revolutionary War in 1793 had seriously affected the Continental market for coal. In any case a shorter and less costly line was mooted, which would link up with the existing wagonway from Pitfirrane. This line was to run, apparently, from a point slightly south-west of the Colton via Urquhart Bridge and Logie. To this effect another contract was drawn up and signed in 1795 with William Hunt, a Dunfermline merchant, who had purchased Logie and Urquhart. Again suitable land was marked out, and this time feu duties were agreed on, but before work commenced the whole plan was abandoned. The reason was that Lord Elgin discovered that the terms of his lease of the Pitfirrane wagonway did not permit him to transport his coal from the pits beyond the Carnock Road which were not leased from Pitfirrane. The feu duties under the agreement remained a bone of contention, as Lord Elgin complained that as the wagonway had not been constructed, nor was now intended, no further feu duties should be paid. Mr. Hunt thought otherwise, and continued to assert his right to them. The argument dragged on in a welter of correspondence, lawyers' letters, counsels' opinions and repeated attempts at arbitration, and had the effect of delaying the completion of a new direct line to Dunfermline for over twenty years, merging into a similar claim to feu duties on Pittencrieff land by Mr. Hunt when he became owner of Pittencrieff in 1800.

Another reason for the delay in construction of a new railway was that Lord Elgin had become involved in public affairs. From 1793 onwards he was ambassador at the courts of the King of Prussia and Austrian Emperor, and from 1799 to 1802 at Constantinople. In addition, on his visits to Broomhall he was engaged, from late 1794, in raising his own regiment, 'The Elgin Fencibles', for service in Ireland. This involved him in considerable expense, for although the Government eventually met his outlays, the payments were several years in arrears. The same situation arose over his official outlays in Constantinople, which were not finally settled until 1809. On his return from the Middle East, he was arrested while passing

20

through France during the temporary peace in 1802, as a reprisal for the alleged mis-treatment of a French General while a prisoner in England. He remained in more or less open arrest until his release in 1806. Only then could he turn his attention finally to completing his railway.

A further complication was that, in addition to bearing the expenses of his official duties, Lord Elgin had spent over £75,000 (possibly more than £1½ million to-day) in collecting the Greek sculptures known as the Elgin Marbles, but had only received £35,000 from a grudging government when he was forced to sell. It says a great deal for his persistence, and the potential value placed on his coal reserves, that he was able to raise enough capital to proceed with the plan for the new direct wagonway which was to reach Dunfermline at last.

As already mentioned, it is possible that this direct line had been under construction from Charlestown from 1795 at least (though no great expenditure is noted in the estate accounts) and by 1809 was approaching the foot of the Pittencrieff Coal Road, from which it was planned to extend it up the Pittencrieff incline to the Coaltown of Pittencrieff (the present Colton) and thereafter to the Baldridge mines.

Unfortunately for the resumption of the scheme agreed with Captain Phyn in 1793, Pittencrieff had been bought in 1800 by William Hunt, who demanded payment of feu duties on the land marked out for the railway by Captain Phyn in 1793, though none had been previously asked or paid. This dispute was added to that over the Urquhart feus. William Hunt died in 1807 but his son and successor William was of like mind (as was his brother James who succeeded in 1810) and the deluge of legal argument continued. It was in fact still simmering well into the middle of the century, by which time the Pittencrieff wagonway had almost outlived its usefulness.

However, a conditional agreement was reached in 1809 so that plans according to the contract of 1793 could be prepared, as this had been held to be binding on the new owner. This agreement has not come to light, but in 1810 John Grieve, an Edinburgh consultant engineer and surveyor much employed by Lord Elgin, prepared a sketch plan showing a double track, between the old Logie Road and the Colton on the western side of the Coal Road. Grieve also envisaged a row of workshops (at the foot of the track) on the Logie Road towards Urquhart Farm for stores and maintenance purposes. Because of the two relatively steep inclines, first to the head of the Coal Road and then, beyond the Crossford road, to the Colton,

Grieve proposed that the line should consist of two gravity inclines or inclined planes, on which the descending laden wagons would pull up the ascending empties by means of an endless rope. Someone, perhaps Lord Elgin, suggested the use of the newly invented steam engine or 'Fire Engine' to assist the haulage. James Hunt objected, and appealed to Lord Meadowbank (who had married the heiress of the Wellwoods). His Lordship upheld Hunt's objection on the grounds that there was no mention of 'Fire Engines' in the original contract of 1793, which was not surprising. In addition to his other proposals, Grieve had included in his plan a row of walled enclosures bordering almost the whole length of the Coal Road, to serve as coal depots for the various pits using the line. Naturally James Hunt objected once more as they would have been too close to his house and policies. As a result, the scheme lapsed again in a morass of legal arguments over the feu duties, the width of the proposed track, the ancillary erections, and anything else which could usefully be brought into the argument. Ten years were to elapse before a railway through Pittencrieff could be built.

Grieve's plan had been prepared in anticipation of the new 'Iron Railway', laid with iron rails instead of wood, reaching the foot of the Coal Road, as construction was well advanced by the end of 1810. It is clear from the increased expenditure appearing in the estate accounts that the construction had begun in earnest in 1809, and had continued while the differences with James Hunt were preventing its possible completion as far as the Colton. This is the railway noted by Fernie in his 'History of Dunfermline' as having reached Dunfermline in 1812, although the terminus at the foot of the Coal Road was not strictly within the burgh boundaries at this period. No techinical details have come to light, but from correspondence of late December 1810 information is available regarding the type of rail being proposed, though there is nothing to show that this was in fact what was laid. Anderson of Leith was offering to supply cast iron rails at £13:15/- a ton, which Lord Elgin considered too dear and offered £13:10/-. At the same time he was seeking estimates for a supply from both Baird and Dixon, the Glasgow ironfounders. The rails were to be 3 feet in length, and capable of bearing a weight of one ton. They were to be 22 lbs. in weight, of a plain wedge shape, 4½ inches deep measured at the mid point of the breadth. Each end had to be perpendicular, fitting into a groove in a stone block to which they were to be bolted, as no sleepers or chairs were to be used. The result of these enquiries is unknown. The length of track was estimated at five to six miles which suggests that their use was confined to the new railway rather

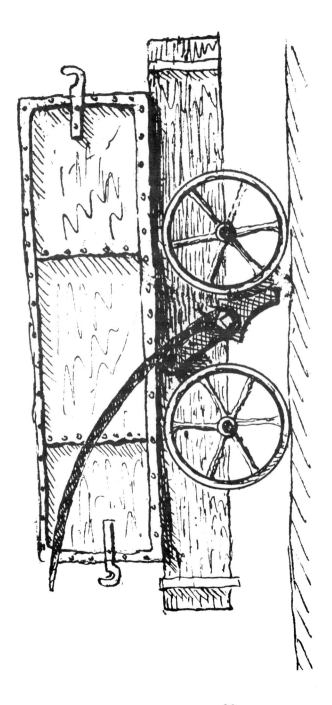

Landale's design for an improved railway wagon, 1820. Note the double acting brake.
Photo The National Museums of Scotland
Elgin Archives

than the old wagonway, which may have continued to use its existing rails.

The cost of building this new and additional railway on a different route was heavy, but once it was completed the advantages outweighed the additional financial burden on the estate. The running costs were to some extent offset by transfers to railway revenue from Colliery accounts to meet a part of wages and maintenance in addition to the free transport of Lord Elgin's coal to Charlestown, which had now replaced Limekilns as the main coal-exporting port in West Fife. The effect of the construction of this new line on coal deliveries at the harbour is illustrated in Note 5. There was further building activity in the years 1817 to 1819, possibly incurred by a partial realignment of the track between Craigs Bank and Meadowend, and the ironing out of curves, as well as laying new tracks from branch lines within the limeworks and collieries. £617 was spent on rails as well as wagon wheels and other ironwork in 1817, a sum which rose to £1,125 in 1819, and £1198 in 1829, largely due to preparations for the last phase to the Colton.

The Pittencrieff Incline

The long saga of the completion of the wagonway link with Dunfermline ended in 1820 when agreement with James Hunt permitted work to start on the controversial inclines to the Colton, despite continued legal wrangling as to whether Lord Elgin had to make retrospective payments of feu duties on the land allocated for the railroad in the agreement with Captain Phyn in 1793. Eventually Counsel found that Mr. Hunt was bound by the letter of that contract and that no feu duties could be exacted.

In any case the completion of the final section of his wagonway was essential to Lord Elgin, as the original line from Crossford which had continued in operation, was now closed. In 1820 Dr. Robertson Barclay of Keavil refused to renew the way-leave for that portion of the line which passed over his ground, thus effectively cutting off the main source of supply to Charlestown, except from the terminus at the foot of the Pittencrieff Coal Road to which all coal from Dunfermline mines had now to be carted.

Robert Stevenson, the engineer grandfather of Robert Louis Stevenson, made a final survey in 1820 of the terrain between the terminus at Pittencrieff Toll and the Colton, and approved the plans, suggesting once again a gravity inclined plane with parallel tracks. This followed the plan put forward ten years earlier by John Grieve which appears to have been the basis of the final construction with the omission of the controversial ancillary erections.

24

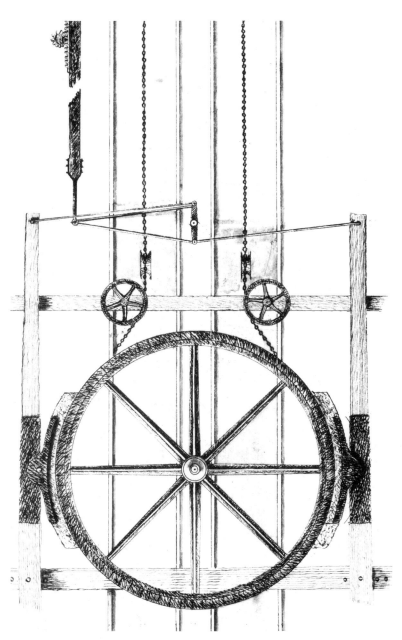

Landale's design for cable wheel at the head of the gravity incline. This or something similar was in use at the Colton. *Photo The National Museums of Scotland*

Elgin Archives

The supervising engineer was Charles Landale of Dundee (Note 6), who had some previous experience in building the Dundee to Newtyle Railway, and who remained in overall charge until the work was completed. The construction proved much more expensive than the earlier works. The cost of a tunnel under the old Logie Road at the foot of the incline, with its cutting, amounted to £1,164 (this is still visible if viewed from the level ground below the road) and a further £1,418 was expended on the remaining portion of the two inclines before the end of 1821, leaving an estimated £655 to be found to complete the project. It is not indicated if these sums included the replacement of the existing rails on the line by the unusual type of 'Edge' rails introduced by Landale on the Colton section (Note 7).

There appears to have been great difficulty in raising enough loan capital to allow the work to proceed smoothly, for at one point, in 1821, the correspondence reveals that Landale was short of money to pay the workmen, and that Mr. McKean, Lord Elgin's agent and accountant in Edinburgh, was trying desperately to secure further loans, promising to send over whatever sums he had in hand so that the work could continue. It was completed by the end of the year.

It is not known whether any mechanical assistance was installed to assist in the haulage on the two inclines. A report in 1838 on the railway and mines mentions three steam engines in use, viz. a 10 hp, a double engine (sic) of 32 hp, and a small one, but these might well have been used at the pits for pumping, though there were three inclines in use at Charlestown, Pittencrieff and the Colton.

The only contemporary description of the new section is contained in one of the 'Prize Essays', written for the Highland Society by Alexander Scott of Ormiston, and printed in the Transactions of that Society in 1829. Although the essay is mainly concerned with methods of raising wagons to different levels, it contains a short description of the 'Elgin' Railway and the method it employed, as well as a description of various types of 'Edge' rails (Note 7). The essay relates: *The Railway on Lord Elgin's works between Dunfermline and Limekilns* (sic) *for design and execution, is inferior to none. On this railway there are two inclined planes, executed with all the requisite machinery for the loaded wagons drawing up the empty ones: the longest of these is about 511 yards, with a declivity of about one in twenty. Between the two inclined planes the ground had been originally level to some extent; and ingenious advantage is taken of this level by commencing at a short distance from the foot of the upper inclined plane, and cutting out a track for a railway*

26

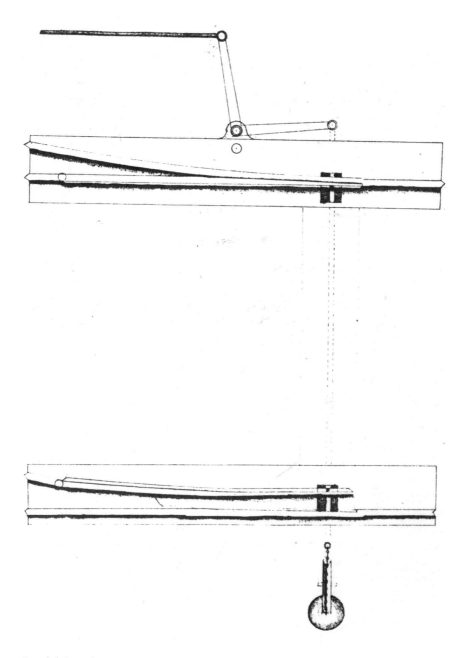

Landale's points on the new railway, 1820.
Elgin Archives   *Photo The National Museums of Scotland*

with an easy slope in the line of the main descending railway for the loaded wagons, by banking up the earth, and facing it with a stone wall; another railway is formed with a similar slope but in a contrary direction, toward the foot of the upper inclined plane. In this manner the two railways are carried forward until they reach the top or bank head of the under inclined plane, where a difference of perpendicular height between the two appears to be about ten feet; the one half of this height gives a declivity to the empty wagons to proceed to the foot of the upper inclined plane; the brake or drag of the loaded wagons has only to be attended to for regulating their motion to the place where they start on the inclined plane.

This description is far from clear, and it is obvious that Alexander Scott did not visit the Charlestown end of the line. It does reveal, however, that there was a raised embankment or embankments between the two planes to enable the loaded wagons to reach the head of the Pittencrieff incline from the Colton without too much loss of momentum although it is difficult to envisage their relationship to the Crossford road which had been constructed through the Urquhart Cut in 1777, and which would have to be crossed by the railway tracks. A portion of the embankment remained until 1895 when it was removed, but Landale's ingenuity had not been enough and eventually horses had to be used to haul the wagons between the two inclines.

Scott, in his article, reveals that the gauge of the railway was 4' 3". In editing the essays Robert Stevenson, who had originally surveyed the track, observed that the 'Edge' rails used by Landale had no iron cross bars, and were raised well above the horse track to prevent them being clogged with earth and dirt. He also states that he personally saw an 11½ cwt. horse pull a load of 23 tons 13 cwt. on these rails.

Although the intention had been to continue the line across the Carnock road beyond the Colton in order to reach Baldridge and Balmule, the only branch immediately constructed was to the James pit to the west of the Colton and north of Berrylaw. Possibly the lack of money was the main factor here, but failure to reach an agreement with Pittencrieff was a contributory cause of delay. By 1830 however the route north had been surveyed and land acquired for the track, which was to run due north of the Colton across the Carnock road and the site of the present Milesmark Hospital. The fact that Spowart of Venturefair, now the lessee of the Wellwood coal pits to the north of Dunfermline, had agreed to build the wagonway at his own expense to meet the main line at Baldridge accounts for the speedy extension. The later accounts show that

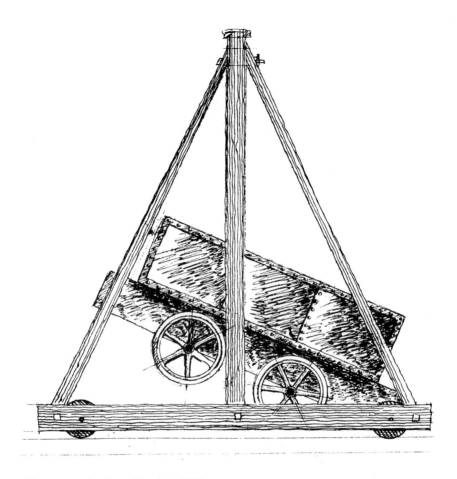

Tipping mechanism, Landale 1820.
Elgin Archives   *Photo The National Museums of Scotland*

Spowart was in need of such an outlet, and his coal freight provided much of the cash income from the line, bearing in mind that Lord Elgin's coal freight was not charged even as a book entry, though payments for maintenance appear in the Colliery accounts.

Passengers and Freight

So far the development of the railway had been motivated by the need to provide a speedy and convenient outlet for the ever-increasing coal output, both for export and the firing of the lime kilns, and throughout the lifetime of the railway this was its main purpose, but such a lucrative trade was built up that lime, limestone, and coal were soon being exported from Charlestown to London, the Continent, and the east coast of Scotland as far as Aberdeen. So many vessels, large and small, were arriving at Charlestown that the harbour had to be extended in 1824, and a sluice constructed to flush out the tidal silt in the inner basin. Landale has left several drawings for a canal for this purpose but the expense prevented these plans from being implemented, though Lord Elgin appears to have toyed with the idea of a canal from Pittencrieff to Charlestown.

About 1830 Lord Elgin had begun to consider the possibility of using his railway to provide an outlet for the spinning and weaving industry, as Dunfermline had limited transport and travelling facilities at this period. As the Colton terminus, and that at the foot of the Coal Road, were a fair distance from the town, he considered building a branch line from the foot of the lower incline to the Nethertown of Dunfermline. He hoped that this would bring greater financial returns from increased freight to offset the interest on capital borrowed to build the railway in the first place.

In fact the simple colliery wagonway had become part of a complicated structure of complementary activities. It was now concerned with freight other than the coal coming down from the Dunfermline area in substantial tonnage, a busy harbour, a small iron foundry producing ironwork for the railway and the pits, extensive lime quarries and kilns, a steam towing company with tug and lighters on the Forth, together with several sloops owned by the estate. Allied to these was an Inn and Sutlery at Charlestown for those waiting for cargo or steam boat, all of which still operated as a part of the normal activities of an agricultural estate. The estate finances had been overstrained by the amount of capital which had had to be borrowed to build and maintain the railway, not to mention the loss on the Elgin Marbles,

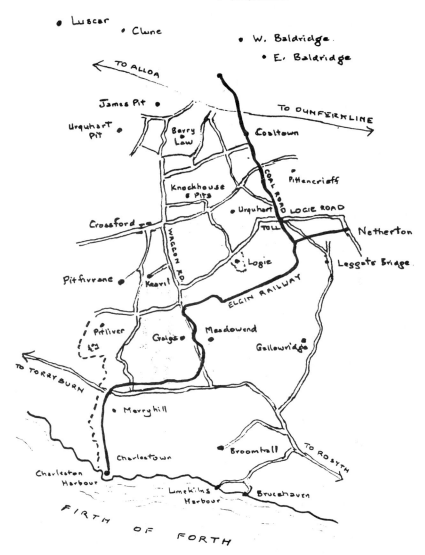

Adapted from a Plan of the Town and Parish of

DUNFERMLINE

The Elgin Railway c.1830 showing places mentioned in text.

Norman Clark

with the result that in 1827 Trustees had been appointed to supervise the estate business, and perhaps act as a check on new ventures. The estate was solvent but there was a debt burden of over £90,000, due to borrowing to finance the expansion of these activities. Nevertheless, though neither the Trustees nor his legal adviser approved, Lord Elgin went ahead with his project which was completed early in 1834. An innovation on this new branch line was the introduction of a horse-drawn passenger coach with seating for fifty passengers. One rumour has it that it was designed by Lord Elgin himself. Towards the end of 1833 this was advertised to leave from the foot of the Coal Road, but the Dunfermline Register for 1834 announced that it would in future leave from the Nethertown terminus, which was situated on the west side of the present Elgin Street. At least two coaches per day were advertised to connect with the Stirling to Granton steamers on the Forth at times depending on the tides. The fare (for the ten to fifteen minute journey to Charlestown) was 6d for an adult, and half-price for children. It was by this coach or its successor that the young Andrew Carnegie with his younger brother and parents left Dunfermline in 1848 to start a new life in America, and from which young Andrew took a long sad look at his beloved Dunfermline.

The inability of the Trustees, meeting infrequently, to control the day to day business of the various branches of the wagonway and its ancillary developments had led them to suggest, as early as 1834, the formation of a public company to relieve the financial pressure and provide adequate management.

Thus in 1836 an optimistic prospectus for the future of the new line was issued by Lord Elgin and his Trustees to attract traffic from the business men and factory owners of Dunfermline now enjoying a boom in linen manufacture:

> *The Line of Railway having lately been surveyed by skilful Engineers, they have given a decided report as to its importance, both in a public point of view for the use of the trade and manufacture of Dunfermline, now so rapidly increasing, and also as affording a most desirable opportunity for the profitable Investment of Capital.*
>
> *The Earl of Elgin and his Trustees have been accordingly induced thus publicly to express their readiness to receive proposals, either from Companies or Individuals, for the aquisition on a tenure of such nature and duration, as may be agreed upon, of this valuable line of Railway in connection with the Port and Harbour of Charlestown, and also, if acquired, with the command*

of such portions of the valuable feuing grounds both at Dunfermline and the coast, and along the line of the Railway, as may be necessary to meet the demands now made both for Dwelling Houses and also for sites for Manufactures, for which the local situation, and the ample supply of water, render it so peculiarly valuable.

For some time past the value and rapidly increasing importance of the line of Railway have been well known. As a Steam Boat Station in the North side of the Forth, Charlestown is without any rival. Although Railway Carriages were only established within the last two years, the number of passengers travelling on this line is already large - amounting during the last season to several hundred a month. With proper exertions and holding out even a moderate share of these facilities, which even the most insignificant stations on the Firth of Clyde enjoy in such abundance, the traffic on this line of Railway in all directions might be immensely increased. Besides the constant intercourse by means of the Stirling and Alloa Steam Boat Companies, a Steam Boat has lately been established between Charlestown and the Chain Pier at Trinity, for the exclusive service of the Charlestown station, and as arrangements will be speedily completed for opening up a large and commodious Pier and Hotel at Charlestown, it is confidently anticipated that the number of passengers will be immediately and very largely increased.

A large and immediate Revenue from the Railway can be at once secured to any parties engaging in this undertaking, even independently of the certain prospect of a rapid increase in the future receipts from it.

It presents an important feature in the proposed undertaking, and one which will in vain be looked for elsewhere, that the whole of this line of Railway, with nearly the whole of the adjacent grounds - the whole of this valuable feuing lands immediately to the south of Dunfermline, for which numerous applications have lately been made for sites for manufactures - the whole ground on the coast, within the Charlestown range, also embracing feuing grounds of the most valuable description, and the entire and exclusive right of property in the extensive port and Harbour of Charlestown, are all held in property by Lord Elgin. Although in this way there is a total freedom from those difficulties which might arise from separate and contending interests, yet in the event of this important undertaking being entered into, in such a way as to promise satisfactory results, Lord Elgin and Trustees will join in carrying a Bill through Parliament for the purpose of facilitating and consolidating the necessary arrangements.

The glowing prospect held out in this prospectus suggests that Lord Elgin and his Trustees were inviting tenders for the purchase, either of shares in a Railway company, or for the outright purchase or lease of the entire railway and harbour, but in the event, the expected support from the Dunfermline factory owners or others outwith the town, did not materialise, nor was any Parliamentary bill sought to turn the undertakings into a public company. In view of the failure of the prospectus to attract interest, the Trustees decided to offer the lease of the railway and harbour to the highest bidder at a public roup. Before this took place, however, John McKean, the Edinburgh accountant, who had been financial adviser to Lord Elgin since before 1820, offered to take over the concern on behalf of the estate. This was accepted.

He agreed to be responsible on behalf of the estate for the payment of all wages and the carriages of goods, including delivery in Dunfermline, for a return of 4d per ton of freight, and 10% of two-thirds of total receipts. The reponsibility for maintenance and policy remained with the Trustees, to whom monthly returns were made via the factor, to be included in the annual estate balance sheet.

In actual fact there was more to his appointment as manager than appears on the surface, for he was practically nominated by the Royal Bank of Scotland to take charge of their interests in the railway as it was a valuable security for substantial loans to the Trustees to maintain the estate and its industries. This arrangement does not seem to have continued beyond McKean's death in 1838 when the Trustees reassumed control.

The Coming of Steam

One would have expected that Lord Elgin, with his enthusiasm for new ventures, would have considered the introduction of a steam locomotive to his railway, at a time when this new invention was attracting so much excitement. In fact as early as 1830 he had actually sampled the experience of travelling on the Liverpool railway behind a steam locomotive (which may well have been

34

Stephenson's 'Rocket') to see things for himself. He was not impressed with the experience. Writing to Joseph Locke, the engineer and backer of George Stephenson, he complained about the unpleasant swinging motion of the carriages. Locke, in reply, explained that this was due to the inclination of the pistons and cylinders on the engine but that modifications were being made to eliminate such movement. Nevertheless the steam locomotive did not replace the horse on the Elgin line for another twenty years, a development which Lord Elgin did not live to see.

However, a considerable amount of freight, apparently articles of small bulk, had been engendered from Dunfermline, apart from the welcome passenger service to Edinburgh via the steamships. The Agent at Dunfermline (whose wage was one guinea per week) soon complained that he needed additional assistance to receive, dispatch, and deliver parcels, not to mention the collection of the fares. The new passenger service proved popular and probably created a new demand, for Dunfermline had only a limited coach connection with Queensferry. In the half year from January to July 1838 6,527 persons travelled to and from Charlestown, and by 1841 the number had risen to 15,763 for the whole year. The recession in the weaving trade, added to a general depression during the 'Hungry Forties', caused the numbers to drop to 9,786 in 1843. Later in 1849 a branch line from the Upper Station at Dunfermline to Crossgates on the Edinburgh, Perth and Dundee Railway offered, perhaps, a more convenient route to Edinburgh - via the Burntisland or Queensferry passage. It is not known whether the provision of special coaches on the Elgin line for the benefit of those who wished to sample the sea bathing at Charlestown did anything to halt the drop in receipts.

Thomas, 7th Earl of Elgin, who had been the driving force behind the expansion of the industrial activities of the estate, died in Paris in 1841, and was succeeded by his son James, the 8th Earl, under whom the next and final expansion took place.

By the 1840s possible deposits of ironstone in West Fife were attracting attention, though in fact these were much less extensive than was believed. At least two iron works were set up, one in Dunfermline, and the other at Oakley. The latter was controlled by John Sligo, who looked to the proposed Stirling to Dunfermline Railway to provide facilities for his new venture. While this was still building, Mr. Sligo suggested in 1840 that he should be provided with a junction at Oakley for his foundry. As a result the projected route between Alloa and Dunfermline was altered to bring the line through a sparsely populated area to serve it. Unfortunately the venture had a short life, and the viability of the railway suffered.

46. *Farther Payments* on account of expense of improving the
Dunfermline & Charlestown Railway Viz:—

1. Price of two Locomotive Engines from Hawthorn & Co.
Leith Engine Works, purchased for _____ 1900

Whereof to be taken by them in coals _____ 475

And formerly paid in part as in Account
ending December 1852. page 9. _____ 725

Deduct _____ 1200

Remains £ 700

Paid to *George C. Bruce C.E.* for purchase of Locomotive Steam Engine
... Railway; per his acknowledgment 24th August 1854 _____ 34 | 875

... for same remitted to him at Newcastle as below, page 11th.

Account to *Neilson & Co*, Hyde Park Foundry, Glasgow, dated 27th Septr
1858, for a Locomotive Tank Engine purchased at the price of £1420 — 17.

Whereof paid 14th December 1858, per receipt & letters from Mr Steedman 710 — 18. 710

Balance for which Bill at 6 mo.
was granted by Mr Steedman £ 710

The cost of the 4 engines used on the railway, 1852-1858.
Elgin Archives   *Photo The National Museums of Scotland*

36

While it was still in operation, with optimistic possibilities, the foundry required outlets farther than Dunfermline, and so by arrangement with the Elgin Railway a spur was led down from the new Stirling-Dunfermline Railway to the Colton Depot, from a point just west of William Street Bridge. Incidentally, when the Stirling railway approached Dunfermline at this point, a wooden bridge carried it over the extension of the Elgin line to Baldridge. When built, this was found to be too low to allow the wagons to pass, and it was replaced by a stone bridge which carried the railway embankment. The entrance to this bridge/tunnel can still be seen, marking the line of the wagonway.

The cost of this junction was met jointly by the Oakley Iron Co. and the Stirling-Dunfermline Railway, and though it meant that freight had to be transferred from railway wagons to the horse-drawn wagons of the Elgin Railway on a different gauge, an increase in the amount of iron carried is noticeable: this necessitated further extensions of the Charlestown line which were long overdue. In 1848 the Trustees and the Iron Co. jointly constructed a circuit to bring a new length of track down to the quays to avoid the steep incline of 1799 from the head of the brae. This involved a new alignment at Merryhill, and opportunity was taken for some adjustment of the line between Meadowend and Craigs Bank (Note 8).

In December 1849 the Trustees at last decided to introduce steam locomotives to replace as far as possible the use of horses, considering that the change would be to their financial advantage, despite having to re-lay the entire track to the railway gauge of $4'8\frac{1}{2}''$ to match that of the Stirling Railway, and alter the wagons to facilitate the changeover at the Colton. In the course of modernisation two bridges were built, one over the Torryburn road and another at Rosebank (Drumtuthil). During 1851 rails and switches to the value of £508 were purchased from John Barclay of Glasgow, while sleepers to replace the stone setts cost £355 from the sawmills of Thomas Harris near Dunkeld, though both firms had to wait more than twelve months for payment.

Thereafter in 1852 two locomotives were purchased from Messrs. Hawthorn of Leith, a branch of the locomotive engineering firm of Newcastle which was one of the main suppliers of locomotives to the North British Railway Co. and other companies springing up at this time. No specifications of these engines have come to light at Broomhall, but it is likely that they were Colliery or Mineral engines designed for work in and around collieries (Note 9). Each cost £950, slightly less than the price charged to the North British for similar types. Of the purchase price, £475 was paid in coal and the remainder in cash, Messrs Hawthorne accepting half-yearly instalments over two years to promote sales. In fact they were still being paid up as late as 1855.

Before the locomotives could be put into passenger service the line had to be inspected and passed by a government surveyor, whose report gives us the details of the railway in 1853. Dated 30th June 1853 it states:-

Dunfermline and Charlestown Railway

Permanent Way: The line is single throughout with sidings as follows:- No. 1 at Commencement of line (or top of incline at Charlestown), in length about 8 chains. No. 2 at 49 chains, about 2 chains in length. No. 3 at 2 miles 67 chains to Engine Shed. and No. 4 at termination of the line. Nos. 2 and 3 are locked.

The Railway which is constructed on the property of the Right Honourable The Earl of Elgin and Kincardine is constructed on his Lordship's estate from the commencement to 2 miles 66 chains, the ground for the remaining portion of the line (19 chains) has been purchased. The width of the line at formation is 15 feet, the gauge 4'8½"; the rails are 15 feet long, wrought iron, 56 lbs per lineal yard. A diagram is annexed (Note 10).

The chairs are Ransom and May's patent. Joint chair 28 lbs in weight, single chair 22lbs. The rails are fixed with compressed elm keys, and the chairs are fastened to the sleepers by oak Trenails. The sleepers are best larch, average length 10'6" by 10'5½" (sic); they are laid tranversely three feet apart. The Ballast consists of Gravel and broken stones not exceeding 5 ozs. in weight, average depth 18".

The switches are of the ordinary kind made by Yule and Wilkie, Glasgow.

Fences: the fences consist of stone and lime walls, and larch paling and quicks.

Drainage: the drains are partly stone and lime, and partly tiles. There are no stations on the line.

The minimum space to be allowed between the sides of the largest proposed carriage at the level of the windows and any fixed work will be two feet.

The accompanying tables of the railway are necessarily incomplete (these are missing from this copy of the Report) *the original Line having been constructed 80 years ago* and no plans or sections being*

---

*This is incorrect as the line under report was not finally constructed until 1821. The inspector was confusing the line with the earlier wagonway from Crossgates to Limekilns of 1774.

in existence - the gradients are however very easy and there is no work of any magnitude upon the line.

The Tables of Curved and straight portions as well as of Bridges and Level Crossings are correct (also missing). *Tracings of recent alterations in order to render the line suitable for locomotive traffic are forwarded herewith* (No trace has been found of these). *The passenger traffic is inconsiderable, the Line being chiefly used for the conveyance of minerals. It is therefore proposed to restrict the rate of travelling to ten miles per hour. There is only one locomotive on the line, so there is no danger of collisions. A small portion of the line is as yet unfenced, but this is to be proceeded with immediately. As it is entirely through land farmed by the proprietor and always under crop, no danger can arise.*

Platforms are to be erected at each terminus and the passenger traffic is to be carried on by ordinary third class carriages.

There is one interesting point revealed by the report, that the passenger terminus at Charlestown was at the head of the brae, near the present Estate Office, and not at the harbour despite the spur built several years earlier.

Operating Difficulties

One engine went into service above the Colton beyond the Carnock Road, and the other on the Nethertown-Charlestown line. The engines were not easily transferred from one section to another as the Roads Commissioners refused to allow them to cross this road under steam, with the result that the laden wagons from Balmule and Baldridge had still to be drawn by horsepower across the Carnock Road to the Colton and the inclines, and when a transfer of engine did take place it was towed and manhandled across. No engine could operate on the inclined plane, and horses had to be used to bridge the gap between the upper and lower inclines as the following description shows. In fact the inclines were expensive in manpower and maintenance, and consideration had already been given to abandon them altogether. It would also seem from the descriptions of the railway at this time by the Rev. Peter Chalmers in his 'Historical and Statistical Account of Dunfermline', first published in 1844 and expanded in a second volume 15 years later, that there must have been considerable delay at the Colton because of these restrictions. No other contemporary account seems to have been written. He says in 1844:

The coal is conveyed to his (Lord Elgin's) *limeworks and shipping*

39

at Charlestown by a railroad, the two inclined planes of which, near the town of Dunfermline, are much admired and were executed, on a change of the line of the railroad in 1821, under the direction of the late ingenious Mr. Landale of Dundee. The Wellwood coal for exportation is now also conveyed along this railway, which is connected with that Colliery by a branch line. The railway is about six miles in length but longer when the branches to the different pits etc. are taken into account. There are from 100 to 500 tons of coal generally conveyed along it in a day, according to the demand, or the number of vessels lying in the Charlestown Harbour waiting for them.

By 1859 he states:

There have been at times 2,000 tons sent down by the Elgin Railway in a fortnight.

These coals were exported to the Baltic and Mediterranean ports, as well as to France, where they were used almost exclusively by the Paris to Rouen steamboats.

In Vol. 2 of his History, Chalmers (1859) further amplified his description:

There are two inclines on the railroad near to the town of Dunfermline and a third at the shore. The coals are conveyed by a locomotive engine from the pits to the top of the first incline at the Colton station, east end of Golf Drum Street, and from the bottom of it they are drawn a short distance, by horses, to the top of the second incline …… and are afterwards conveyed by another locomotive, which takes also goods and passengers from the Nethertown station in the town of Dunfermline to the steamboats that ply between Stirling and Granton piers.

From this it would appear that the ingenious Mr. Landale's embankments were no longer in use, though they were not removed entirely until 1895.

Mechanical Troubles

Mechanically the locomotives were not an unqualified success, as the existing documents reveal a continual need for maintenance and repair involving replacement of parts, particularly wheels and brakes, and new copper fireboxes. Engine wheels had to be sent from Leith, being collected by lorries which went round by Stirling. There are no references to deliveries by sea, except for one wagon. Wagon wheels wore out quickly, and had to be recast at Charlestown Foundry, while a Dunfermline blacksmith figures frequently in the accounts for running repairs, mainly to the engines.

In 1855 nearly £200 had to be spent on the Charlestown engine, and £185 in 1858, no doubt with similar sums in other years. Nevertheless two further locomotives were purchased, one in 1854 on the recommendation of Messrs. Bruce and Cunningham, Engineers, Edinburgh at a cost of £875 which suggests that it was second-hand, and the other in 1858 for £1,420 from Neilson of Glasgow, who may have built the earlier engine. It is desribed as a Tank engine (Note 9). It is not known where these were employed though it is likely they were mainly used within the collieries and on the northern section of the line. Earlier in 1855 Mr. George Bruce was called in to find the cause of so many breakdowns, and his report reveals the main faults in the engine construction. Their wheels had cast iron spokes with case hardened, wrought iron tyres, and on both the upper and lower sections of the track spokes were snapping with unfailing regularity. Mr. Bruce suggested that this was due to excessive braking on the gradients from Balmule which caused uneven expansion between the tyres and the spokes. It was pointed out, however, that the same was happening on the run to Charlestown where the level track required practically no braking. No other explanation was offered however.

The enginemen also complained that the end of the cylinder rusted in its socket, and required to be cleared by pressure from the piston rod to remove the packing. The reply was that the cylinder case ought to be inspected every morning, and clean clay placed round the inside of the iron door to prevent draught, thus preventing the ignition of any residue of coal and ashes while in motion, which does not seem to answer the original complaint. Unspecified pumps had also to be examined every day. As for the brakes which were wearing rapidly, thin strips of brass were to be inserted daily in the brakes, as well as in motion bars, eccentric pulley, eccentric strap, and crankshaft to take up the wear.

A further difficulty was the design of the boiler, the fore part of which tended to dry out when ascending an incline with unfortunate results or loss of power. All that could be said on this point was that sufficient amount of water should be kept in the boiler at all times.

Despite the original restriction to ten miles an hour by the government inspector, the speed limit was further reduced to eight miles per hour on the straight, and six on the curves, partly to reduce wear and tear to the locomotives, and partly because of damage to the wagons and their wheels. The latter were constantly developing 'flats' due to the practice of 'scotching' the wheels, i.e. locking them with a pin at the head of the incline. In 1854, 743 wheels were

Brought forward £11,823 | 9 | 6¾

Payments in account of the Expenses of improving the
Dunfermline & Charlestown Railway, Viz:—

1. Account to Thomas Harris Inverkeithing Saw mills, for
4,067 Sleepers for Railway paid 29th September £355 17 3 | 65
1852. per same discharged with certificate & receipt.

2. Sum in Bill to John Barclay, Glasgow, for rails
and Switches dated 1st April 1861. at 18 months 568 4 10 | 66
retired 4th October 1852.

3. Price of two locomotive engines from Hawthorns
& Co. Leith Engine Works purchased for 1,200 . .
Whereof to be taken by them in coals— 475 . .
Remains 725 . .
In part whereof three Bills were grant-
=ed, for the respective sums of £250.
£260. & £225. all dated 27th June 725 - . 725 . . | 67
1852. and at 6 months. paid 16th | 68
July 1852. per said Bills retired— | 69

Remains due of the price 500

And for which Sum of £500 three Bills were
granted, all dated 6th May 1852 at 6 months for
£250. 1/50 & £200 respectively.

Sum 1,589 | 2 | 1

The cost of steam engines, rails etc. for the new railway, 1852.
Elgin Archives   *Photo The National Museums of Scotland*

42

required as replacements, almost double what had been required in 1847, Poor quality castings were blamed, but screw brakes were to be fitted despite the objections of the men working the wagons, on the grounds that they were too slow to apply in an emergency.

Curves were apparently so tight on the upper part of the line that wagons were being damaged by the failure of the buffers to meet when the wagons telescoped on a bend. Extra blocks of wood had to be fixed to each end of the wagons to prevent damage to the frame.

The Financial Burden

The accounts for the period of reconstruction necessitated by the introduction of steam engines between 1850 and 1855 show that it was a costly business, which put a severe strain on the resources of the railway by increasing the amount of borrowed capital. Some of this has already been indicated. The total expenditure over the five years amounted to at least £13,000, bringing the burden of debt to £25,226, involving an annual interest charge of £2,809. On the surface this appears to be in excess of the net revenue of the railway before charging interest, but it is difficult to get a true picture as the cash income came mainly from freight on coal from Balmule, worked by Messrs. Spowart, which in 1854 amounted to 29,839 tons at 1/6d per ton. Further income for a time was derived from freight to and from the Oakley Iron Co. as well as from declining passenger receipts and harbour dues. On the other hand the coal from Lord Elgin's pits at Baldridge and Rosebank was sent down free of charge, amounting to some 90,000 tons for export for the same period, but only a proportion of the running costs of the railway was charged to the Colliery account.

On balance it would seem that the railway was barely solvent, and was possibly being subsidised by revenues from coal sales. There are signs, however, that the output from Lord Elgin's pits was declining by mid century and in consequence the revenue from coal sales fell. As a result the Trustees were forced to look closely at the viability of the railway and to consider whether it could continue to be run by the estate as a private company. (Note 11).

The Final Years

The early nineteenth century has been described as a period of 'Railway Mania' when numerous small independent lines proliferated in isolation, This led to the growth of large companies which absorbed the local lines to form a connected railway system, companies such as the two main rivals in Scotland, the North British and the Caledonian Railways, which expanded rapidly by buying up these local lines to form a network of continuous lines with industrial and commercial potential. So far, the early industrial potential of West Fife had been dependent on the Elgin line, although there was another small wagonway between Townhill and Halbeath by 1812, and as early as 1770 Sir Robert Henderson of Fordell had built one from his Fordell Colliery to St. Davids (Note 1).

In 1856, however, yet another railway for West Fife was proposed, intended to tap the relatively undeveloped coal deposits to the northeast of Dunfermline. The new company, calling itself the West of Fife Mineral Railway, proposed building a single track along Loch Fitty to Kelty, and eventually linking up with the Edinburgh, Perth, and Dundee Railway. At the Dunfermline end, it was to join the Stirling to Dunfermline Railway, and so have access to the Elgin Railway and Charlestown. Its promoters claimed that as 200,000 tons of coal were already being exported from St. David's, Inverkeithing, and Charlestown each year, they could provide a more convenient (and profitable) means of transport from the Kelty/Loch Fitty area. As the prospectus stated:

It is proposed to construct a railway to commence by a junction with the Stirling to Dunfermline Railway, the Elgin, and the Edinburgh Perth and Dundee Railways at Dunfermline, and to be carried through Burgh lands to the Loch Fitty coalfield, and thence by Roscobie Limeworks to a central point in the Saline Ironstone district beyond Redcraigs, from which first diversion of the works, near Balmule, it is further proposed to carry the railway along the margin of Loch Fitty, in the line best calculated to accommodate the mineral field intervening between that and Blairadam, and by Kelty onwards to Kinross .... The Railway is proposed to be formed with a single line only; it is calculated that the cost of construction should not exceed £4,000 per mile.

The new company was incorporated by Act of Parliament in 1856, and James, 8th Earl of Elgin, became a major shareholder, although he had not been one of the original promoters. It was obvious that such a railway serving new pits would greatly add to the traffic on the Elgin line, and a close association of the two lines would make sound commercial sense (Note 13). Construction of the new line began in 1859, not at Dunfermline, but at Kingseat Farm south of Loch Fitty, initially proceeding westwards south of Loch Fitty, south of Highholm Farm to a point just west of Lillyhill. Thereafter it ran north via Muirside, Lochead Toll and Dunduff. Part of the construction can still be seen behind the former Dunduff school, and the bridge carrying this section over the road has only recently been removed. It eventually joined the Stirling to Dunfermline Railway by a bridge across the Carnock Road beyond Rumblingwell, now dismantled, while a reconstructed branch gave access to the Colton. The line was also extended south of Loch Fitty to join the main line at Kelty Station. It is not known how much of the track laying and bridge building was done by the West of Fife Co. before 1863 or whether most was the work of the North British Railway after that date, though it seems that the West of Fife Co. had bought at least one engine from Neilson of Glasgow between 1856 and 1863 (Note 9).

Though there was increased tonnage from Spowart's pits, the decline in passenger receipts, the loss of the Oakley Iron Co. freight, and reduction in demand for lime had reduced the profitability of the Elgin railway and harbour. Both railway and harbour required modernisation, and the inclined planes at Pittencrieff were seen to be an expensive hindrance to the increased traffic expected. Steps would have to be taken to remove them (Note 12). For these reasons Lord Elgin and the Trustees of the Broomhall estate decided that the capital outlay involved in modernising the railway and harbour was prohibitive, despite the optimistic forecast of coal production and returns from freight contained in the preliminary surveys of the potential of the new areas to be opened up (Note 13). They therefore began to consider their future relationship with the new company and, meanwhile, to facilitate any such arrangements, procured an Act of Parliament to incorporate the Elgin Railway as a public company, which was ratified in 1859. Once the relationship of the Elgin Railway to the Royal Bank, the principal creditor, was adjusted, negotiations were opened with the West of Fife Railway for the outright sale of the Elgin Railway and Charlestown Harbour, which took place in 1861. Four locomotives (only one with a tender), two passenger coaches, two coal trucks (in lieu of tenders), two hundred and fifty wagons, one covered van, permanent way, the harbour and all its installations were valued at £70,000, which was eventually paid by the North British Railway Co. when they in turn bought over the West Fife Mineral Railway

Co. in 1863. Having acquired the Edinburgh, Perth and Dundee Railway, and the Stirling to Dunfermline Railway, the North British had rounded off its holdings to give it a consolidated railway system which effectively excluded its rival, the Caledonian Railway, from Fife. Although the West Fife Railway retained its identity for a time for purposes of accounting, the Elgin Railway as a part of Broomhall estate came to an end in July 1863.

Several changes took place immediately. Ground between Elbow End, near Leggats Bridge, and the foot of the New Row was acquired by the North British Railway Co. to build a new line from a point at the east end of Comely Park, Dunfermline, at which it would join a new circuit under construction from the Upper Station which had been the town's first station in 1849. This approach necessitated a viaduct across the New Row which was begun in 1864. Incidentally when the Provost's Committee of Dunfermline Town Council examined the plans in March 1864 it insisted on a much wider span across the road, thus preventing a major traffic problem nearly a century later.

Passenger services from the Netherton ceased and were only resumed from the Comely Park Station in 1894 when the Charlestown-Limekilns station was opened, and continued to run until that station was closed and dismantled in 1926. Modern bungalows now occupy the site and the track. The Netherton terminus remained as a coal depot until fairly recently, served by the 1834 line from the foot of the Coal Road, though the sharp curve there necessitated the use of a short base 'Pug' engine.

The opening of the connecting line between the Upper and Lower stations also rendered the Colton depot and inclined planes obsolete though they appear to have been retained in part until 1875 at least for wagon storage, but coal traffic had long ceased by that date. Only the pit for the winding machinery, the tunnel under the entrance and the railway spur remain visible.

The present Lower Station, originally Comely Park Station, was not officially opened until 1877, but passengers to the ferries would have been able to reach Queensferry or Burntisland via Crossgates from the Upper Station. However by that date a direct connection between Dunfermline and Queensferry had become available. A line was begun from the Ferry by a new company formed, appropriately enough by the Earl of Elgin, in 1873, which was bought out almost immediately by the North British Railway to maintain its monopoly. This had probably led to the construction of a proper station at its proposed terminus at Dunfermline.

Some rebuilding and realignment of the track to Charlestown

appears to have been carried out. A new line was later to branch off from the Elgin line beyond Elbow Junction to link Dunfermline with Kincardine and Alloa, a line which is still in use, serving the 'merry-go-round' coal trains from Seafield, Kirkcaldy, to Longannet Power Station at Kincardine. A further extension of the Elgin line was taken to Crombie Naval Base just before or during the 1914-18 War, following mainly the old route.

And so the story ends. No passenger trains now run from Dunfermline to Charlestown and its harbour, which has long ceased to operate. During the latter half of the 19th century other more convenient ports were developed by the North British, and other more profitable pits were opened. The lime works finally closed in 1936, but the output had been declining for many years previously, as lime was no longer in such demand. By 1914 the North British Railway Co. was considering the complete closure of the harbour, but the 1914 War gave it a reprieve. It continued to be used for small craft, and provided a refuge for small vessels during the last war. To-day a few pleasure craft occupy the basins once packed with foreign and coastal shipping awaiting their cargoes of lime or coal, and modern villas and bungalows encroach upon the lime quarries, the coal depots, and the railway line to which the harbour largely had owed its existence.

NOTES

Note 1: The two authorities for the early Scottish wagonways are 'Early Railways in Scotland and Ireland' by Dendy Marshall, and a pamphlet on Scottish Colliery wagonways by David Dott (1947), neither of which is reliable on dates or facts concerning the Elgin railway, because of the lack of relevant documents at the time of writing. The earliest Scottish colliery wagonway was that between Tranent and Cockenzie laid down in 1722: its wooden rails were replaced by iron ones in 1816, and it was in use until 1886. The Earl of Mar built a line from Sauchie to Alloa Harbour in 1769 with wooden rails: it was in operation on iron rails until 1926. Sir Robert Henderson of Fordell built a line of wooden rails from Fordell Colliery to St. Davids about 1770 (Dott says 1752, but that seems too early): the line was laid with iron rails in 1836, and remained in operation with many alterations until 1946. The other local line was from Halbeath to Inverkeithing, built in 1781-1783: it got its iron rails in 1811, but was abandoned in 1867. The Balmule and Townhill lines are referred to in the text.

Note 2: George Chalmers was born in Banffshire c.1720, but was settled in Edinburgh by 1744. He soon became a burgess and member of the Merchant Company, becoming a recognised figure in the business as well as the social and cultural life of the city. He had many successful and unsuccessful ventures, being described as a banker, coal master, grain dealer, importer from Spain and America, organiser of postal services in the Highlands. In addition he was in 1767 Commissioner for the Convention of Royal Burghs to meet with John Smeaton to draw up plans for a Forth and Clyde Canal, which were disowned in 1778 and he lost his claim for his expenses. At this time he was also Assessor for Fife ports for the Convention and had purchased in 1765 the estate of Pittencrieff with Gowkhall and Baldridge, rich in coal deposits, which he had hoped to export through his newly acquired port of Brucehaven. He also owned other coal deposits near Falkirk and property on the High Street of Edinburgh. It is suggested he anticipated Sir John Sinclair's Board of Trade and the Old Statistical Account.

In Dunfermline, despite his failure to acquire a monopoly of the coal industry, he built at his own expense a new approach road to the town from the south, as well as extending the High Street by a bridge with houses and shops, possibly in consultation with Smeaton. In gratitude the Town Council had his portrait painted by Raeburn, which now hangs in the Council Chambers.

He had over-reached himself and became bankrupt in 1782, suffering a judicial sale of his properties, many local coal deposits being bought or leased by Thomas, Lord Elgin.

Chalmers died in Edinburgh in reduced circumstances.

Note 3: The disposal of Pittencrieff Estate

The estate was broken up and sold in August 1784. The house and grounds were eventually bought by Captain Phyn but the mineral rights on Mounthooly, Drumtuthill (Rosebank), East Luscar, Clune, Gowkhall and Baldridge were bought by a John Gordon on behalf of Ramsay of Barnton, the pioneer of long-distance coaches, and Patrick Miller of Dalswinton, who put one of the first steamships on Dalswinton Loch. Miller acquired Ramsay's portion, and sold the whole in 1790 to the Earl of Elgin for £4,200 (Decreet of Sales 15th December 1785).

Note 4: The following table of the cost of timber for rails, wagons, etc. for the years 1808 to 1811 reveals the expense of upkeep.

Timber for Rails		Timber for Wagon Repairs
1808	£325: 7:4	£630:16:8
1809	£273:12:0	£549: 5:2
1810	£799:11:6	£1,180: 3:2
1811	£789: 2:6	£288: 6:6

Part of this expense was due to the modernisation and building of a new track to Dunfermline.

Note 5: The improvements bringing the line nearer to Dunfermline, and so providing an outlet for the mines north of Dunfermline led to a massive increase in the tonnage delivered at Charlestown as the following table illustrates. Export of coal from Limekilns must have ceased by 1820 with the closure of the original wagonway which initially reduced the tonnage exported.

Coal and limestone delivered to Charlestown by the Elgin Railway

	Coal	Limestone	
1804	13,846 tons	not known	By original wagonway
1819	44,008 tons	52,800 tons	By old and new lines
1820	50,502 tons	58,493 tons	By both lines
1821	49,973 tons	35,325 tons	By new line only

The above output came almost entirely from the mines owned or leased by Lord Elgin, and from his own quarries. It would appear that the sale of limestone reached its peak in the second decade of the 19th century, though production was to continue into the present century. The figures should be compared with those quoted in Note 11. When the railway reached the Pittencrieff Coal Road in 1812, a contract was signed with the Dunfermline Townhill Coal Company which had been formed by Thomas Scotland, Matthew Parker, a Mr. Renwick and others to operate the Townhill Colliery. The contract gave the Dunfermline Coal Co., as it was called, leave to export Townhill coal to Edinburgh and Leith via the Charlestown railway, and gave it the selling rights of Lord Elgin's own coal there. This scheme and the company seems to have collapsed by 1814 as Lord Elgin complained that the company was failing to promote his coal and was undercutting it in favour of their Townhill coal.

Note 6: Charles Landale of Dundee; Very little is known of this early Scottish railway engineer, though a study of his work is apparently being undertaken. He had left at Broomhall a book of sketches of double tracks, haulage machinery, tipping mechanism for coal wagons, a new type of wagon and a possible canal, some of which are shown in the text. He may have remained in the district, residing at North Queensferry, for a house said to have been his was later destroyed by fire. He was deceased by 1849. Another Landale, possibly a son, had interests in local coal mining in the latter half of the century.

Note 7: The term 'Edge Rails' was used in the early 19th century to describe a type or types of iron rail which replaced the original flat iron plates used in some of the early wagonways. The Highland Society Prize Essays contain several references to these innovations, particularly in the essay by George Robertson of Bowes Lodge, Ayrshire. He describes three different types, and the illustration drawn by Landale, and preserved at Broomhall, presumably illustrates another form of the same installed on the new Iron Railway in 1820.

According to Robertson, the first rails were flat and slightly convex, being laid flat with the ground, while the wagon wheels were concave. Derailments were frequent due to dirt and stones falling on the rail. The new type to which he gave the name 'Edge Rail' was a cast iron rail, convex in section with a ridged edge, in which ran a concave wheel, not apparently flanged. He gives various illustrations.

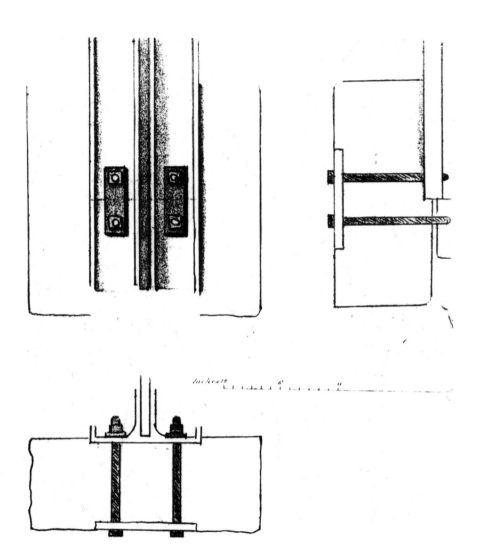

Landale's 'Edge' Rails, 1820.
Elgin Archives *Photo The National Museums of Scotland*

Fig. 1.   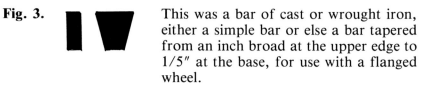   An example of early flat rail.

Fig. 2.   This was a bar of cast or wrought metal 28 lbs. in weight, which was set on edge. The wagon wheel and not the rail was now flanged.

Fig. 3.   This was a bar of cast or wrought iron, either a simple bar or else a bar tapered from an inch broad at the upper edge to 1/5″ at the base, for use with a flanged wheel.

Fig. 4.   The type installed by Landale is illustrated in the text.

We do know that these early pre-Landale rails were anchored to stone blocks, a few of which have survived at Broomhall. Landale's drawing suggest that his rails were first laid on a flat plate, and bolted to stone setts, but the examples of the stone blocks at Broomhall show only one hole suitable for a wooden plug, suggesting that they belong to the 1811 rather than the 1820 installation of iron rails.

In his essay Alexander Scott describes the common method of fixing the rails. These were slightly broader at each end to allow them to lie solidly on the stone blocks, and to add to their strength were raised along their centres. They were four feet in length, while the block was normally 9 to 12 inches thick, and a foot square, with a hole bored in the centre to a depth of six inches, into which an oak plug was driven. Each rail had a square notch in the centre of both ends about half an inch on each side, somewhat narrower below. When the ends of two rails were placed together over the hole in the block, a hole of one inch sides was formed through which a counter sunk nail was driven into the oak plug. The horse track between the rails was filled with road metal up to the sole of the rail, nearly up to the flange on the wheels. Stevenson in his editorial commented on Lansdale's innovation of raising the rails above the level of the ballast track. (The Transactions of the Highland Society Vol, 6 1824).

Note 8: There appear to have been several realignments from time to time, usually when a major change took place as in 1820. The track above Craigs Bank in Henderson's map of 1838 shows a decided kink which does not appear in later maps. A completely new section of track, at Meadowend, was certainly constructed, possibly in 1820 or when locomotives were being introduced. No reasons have been found, though ironing out of curves or better foundations may have been the cause. Other modifications took place in the same area in 1846 and 1851. The North British also made modifications to the original line after 1863, as well as building the present access from the Lower Station, but, by and large, the line was basically that of the wagonway of 1820.

Note 9: Some rather confusing details of what must be the Elgin engines are contained in a booklet published by The George Stephenson Society, entitled 'Locomotives of the North British Railway', compiled from lists kept at the Locomotive works of the North British at Cowlairs. Unfortunately the records seem confused, and some dates ascribed to the early engines taken over from the West of Fife Mineral Railway and Elgin Railway in 1863 by the North British cannot be correct. Five engines are listed, but only four belonged to the Elgin Railway. Three of these can be tentatively identified, and one positively. It looks as though the West of Fife Railway had itself bought a Neilson engine between 1859 and 1863. The three Elgin engines of which one can be reasonably sure are listed in the above booklet as follows:-

No. 163 (North British number) A Hawthorn of Leith engine. An 0-4-2- with 14 x 18 cylinders and coupled four feet six inch wheels. Definitely said to have been built for the Charlestown Railway in 1857. This date should be 1852 as no Hawthorn engine was purchased after that date and this must be one of the two original engines. It was rebuilt in 1866 as an 0-6-0 with 13 x 18 outside cylinders, and was in service until 1891.

No. 164 A Hawthorn 0-4-0 with 12 x 18 cylinders dated correctly as 1852. It was a small engine with a five feet four inch wheelbase and coupled four inch wheels. It is described as a tank engine when sold to a Monklands Colliery, but earlier had been termed a tender engine.

No. 165 An 0-4-0 Neilson dated 1858-1859, with 14 x 18 cylinders. In 1867 it was described as a tender engine, but also as a saddle tank. It is said to have been built for the Elgin Colliery, and if this is correct it must be the engine bought in 1858. It remained in service

Note 10: Section of rail laid in 1851 for the introduction of steam locomotives as contained in the official report of the government inspector 1852. A short section used as a support for a basement floor in a Dunfermline house has been measured and confirms the accuracy of the section illustrated.

Section of Rail
56 lbs. per Yard

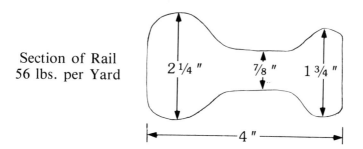

Note 11: The following table from returns extracted from Broomhall Account books illustrated the profitability of the line and harbour at various times. The trade and industrial recession of the 1840s dealt a severe blow from which the line did not recover to any great degree. The decline in the pasenger traffic is notable. The coal traffic was wholly from Messrs. Spowart's pits to the north of Dunfermline as Lord Elgin's coal does not figure in the later returns.

Traffic	Gross Returns	Nett Profit	Total Profit
1838 (six months)			
Coal 11,670 tons	£1,252: 1:10½	£806: 3: 3½	
Passengers (6,527)	£154: 2: 3	£24:18:10	
Freight	£180: 4: 6½	£22:12: 0½	£853:14:2
1841 Coal (33,972)	£3,674:19: 9	£2,129:11: 2	
Passengers (15,763)	£367:17: 6	£250:19: 0	
Freight	£377:10: 7	....	£2,380:10:2
1842 Coal (22,033)	£2,387: 5:11	£1,374:15:10	
Passengers (15,537)	£355:15: 9	£175: 6: 9½	
Freight	£239: 3: 3	......	£1,550: 2:7½
1843 Coal (23,283)	£2,574: 3: 7	£1,396:17:10	
Passengers (9,786)	£277: 6: 3	£113: 8: 3	
Freight	£175: 6: 2	......	£1,510: 6:1½

Traffic	Gross Returns	Nett Profit	Total Profit
1854 Coal (29,839)	£2,237:18: 6	£837: 4: 9½	
Passengers	£245:11: 8	£29: 4: 5½	
Freight	£1,454: 8: 3	£364: 8: 7½	
Charlestown	£556: 0: 0	£423:17: 5½	
Harbour	(No entry.	Concealing a loss?)	
			£1,654:15:4
1861 Coal and Freight (79,755)	£4,314: 4:11	....	
Passengers (5839)	£123: 4: 0	....	
Harbour	£253: 6: 7	....	

The output from Lord Elgin's pits appears to be declining, either from exhaustion or difficulty of working. The Colliery Accounts for 1860 give a tonnage of 43,123, a drop from 56,870 tons in 1842. In 1861 it declined further to 36,155: this is reflected in the harbour profits. The report of 1859 reveals that the railway had lost all the freight from the Oakley Iron works to the West of Fife Railway.

Note 12: The Report to the Trustees 15th December 1859.

'Statement of Works required to be done to make the railway capable of an Increase of Traffic'

First - The removal of the self-acting incline at a cost of £3,000
Second - The improvement of the machinery at the Pittencrieff Incline *   £500
Third - The temporary improvement of the Charlestown Incline £200

Fourth - The removal of several old buildings at Charlestown Harbour, the rearrangement of the rails and shipping apparatus, and the erection of one tipping staithe in the new harbour £500

Say, £6,500

*This seems to be at variance with the previous item, unless some other means of haulage was envisaged, or was included as an alternative to closure.

The final total given in the report seems to contain a generous allowance to provide for underestimation!

'These improvements are essential and might be carried out forthwith, as they will enable the company to carry as much traffic as the harbour in its present state can conveniently accomodate, and the saving on working expenses will more than cover the Interest on outlay, without taking into account the profit to be derived from an increase in traffic.'

Note 13: Table showing the anticipated increase in traffic arising from the formation of the West of Fife Mineral Railway and its connections.

(The totals bear little relation to the sum of the individual estimates and may be not a true total but only another 'guesstimate'.)

1st	Lassodie Mineral Field 28,000 tons @ 1/-	£1,000
	Lessee Jas. Spowart (pits now sinking)	
2nd	Kingseat and part of Townhill 15,000 tons @ 1/-	£750
	Lessee Henderson,	
	Wallace & Co. (now sinking)	
3rd	Kelty Collieries (going pits) 15,000 @ 1/-	£750
	Lessee the Earl of Moray	
4th	Lochgelly 30,000 tons @ 9d	£1,125
	Lessee the Lochgelly Iron Co.	
	(going pits)	
5th	The Hill of Beath 10,000 tons @ 1/-	£500

Lessee Mr. Ord Adams
(field lately bought and about to be worked extensively)

Total from the West of Fife Railway, who will have to give back their Oakley traffic to Charlestown which at present they take to Alloa. £4,500

From the Forth Iron Co. 30,000 tons @ 9d	£1,125
From the Pig Iron 30,000 tons @ 9d	1,125
	£2,250

Or altogether £6,750 of which about £4,000 must be considered clear profit.

INDEX